Finding My Pure Heart Again

By Angie Marino-Smith

Copyright © 2010 by Angie Marino-Smith

Finding My Pure Heart Again
by Angie Marino-Smith
Cover design by Josh Mitchell

Printed in the United States of America

ISBN 9781609573805

All rights reserved solely by the author. The author guarantees all contents are original and do not infringe upon the legal rights of any other person or work. No part of this book may be reproduced in any form without the permission of the author. The views expressed in this book are not necessarily those of the publisher.

Unless otherwise indicated, Bible quotations are taken from The Student Bible NIV. Copyright © 1986, 1992 by Zondervan Publishing House.

www.xulonpress.com

Table of Contents

Chapter One-Getting Noticed 11
    The Beginning 12
    Starting Over 13
    Big Mistake 14
    Mistake Number Two 17

Chapter Two-Being in Love 20
    Mr. Perfect 21
    Mr. Perfect and Me 23
    Is this a Problem? 24
    Too Close for Comfort 25
    The Sin 26

Chapter Three-Relationship Broken 31
    God Noticed Me 32
    Picking Up the Pieces 36
    The first Stephen 37
    …And the Other Stephen 38

Chapter Four-Alone With God 41
    Perfect Time to Ponder 41
    A Glimpse Into a Godly Man's Heart 43
    One Starry Night 48

Chapter Five-Answered Prayer 52
    Climbing Upward 53
    The Return of the Boyfriend in England 54
    Let the Games Begin 56
    A Mother's Intuition 57

Chapter Six-The Battle and the Proposal 61
    The Letter 62
    The Engagement 65
    Preparation for the Body, Mind and Soul 66

Chapter Seven-An October Wedding 69
    My Prince, Where is He? 72
    You May NOW Kiss the Bride 73

Chapter Eight-Great Smokey Mountains
and Ten Years After 76
    Cabin on the Mountaintop 77
    My Guilty Conscience 79
    Intimacy 81

Chapter Nine-The Topic of Sex 84
    Just a Bunch of Old Women Talking
        about Sex 85
    Making Sense of It All 89
    The Huge Ugly Weed 90

Chapter Ten-The Joy of Sex Revealed 93
    Wrapped in a Red Ribbon 94
    Our New Life 95
    My Pure Heart 97

Acknowledgments

My deepest thanks to those who helped me find myself again. To my amazing husband, David, who believes in my dreams and supports them fully (even when they seem crazy). To my beautiful daughters, Abigail and Isabelle, I pray that you will always seek out God's path for your lives and follow the true lover of your souls. To Emily, who encouraged me to speak on purity even before I knew I had something to say. To Joy, who gently prompted me to listen to the "old women talk about sex," your faithfulness to the Spirit's leading changed my life. Laurie, thank you for praying for me since I was a young, shy girl in your Sunday school class. To Lindsey, thank you for helping me to edit this project, I know it took some serious work. I appreciate your wisdom and guidance. To my dearest, "bestest" friends of all, Dan and Jen, thanks for helping me to see that my story needed to be told and for encouraging me to move forward. Mom and Dad, thank you for raising me in a Christian home and teaching me about the Lord. And to my true love, my God and Savior, who loves me today, yesterday and tomorrow, thank you for guiding me and pushing me with your gentle words to write this book.

Introduction

When I kept silent, my bones wasted away through my groaning all day long. For day and night your hand was heavy on me; my strength was sapped as in the heat of summer. Then I acknowledged my sin to you and did not cover up my iniquity. I said, "I will confess my transgressions to the Lord"—and you forgave the guilt of my sin.
- Psalm 32: 3-5

God began working in my life several years ago. At first, I did not listen. I was caught up in the busyness of day-to-day life, and I did not realize that He was trying to get my attention. For years, I didn't want to face the mistakes buried in my past, and I hid them from the people I loved the most. God had a different plan. He wanted to use my past, my shame, my inadequacy for His glory. This book was written because of Him, the Warrior that took my sin, nailed it to a cross, and helped me find my pure heart again. Journey with me and, together, we'll find the pathway to purity and healing. Your heart can be whole again.

Chapter One

Getting Noticed

He was a football player, and he was also popular. I was the new kid on the block. When he started paying attention to me I was stunned! "Is he looking at me?" I asked my friend who had known him for several years.

"Yes, he is totally interested in you. He wants to ask you to the dance," she replied.

"What? He wants to ask me to the dance? He's so cute and he could ask anyone…why me?" I wondered. He started towards us, threading his way through the tables that covered the main floor of the library. "Oh no! How should I act? I'm going to mess this one up I just know it! I mean look at him!" I whispered.

"Hey, I don't think we've met yet," he said with a smile.

"Uh…yeah. I'm Angie," I nervously replied.

"Hi Angie," he said. As they say, it was history from that point on. The handsome, popular football player and I became an item and everyone called us the "cutest couple in school."

The Beginning

Let's go back a couple of years. Not many guys noticed me. I was shy, had long, brown hair, and wore a private school uniform complete with a dorky pair of glasses. My parents sent me to Christian school from kindergarten through seventh grade, so my wardrobe was definitely not trendy. When my parents decided it was time for public school, my mom and I had a blast throwing out the uniforms and going shopping. I got contacts and a new haircut. I was ready to trade-in my shy personality and out-of-style look for a whole new me!

Junior high was rough. Even though I was getting more attention from the boys, they still made fun of me. One day in art class, the teacher stepped out of the room for a minute, and a boy sitting next to me grabbed my purse right from my hand. He started looking through the different compartments and pulling stuff out. This normally wouldn't have been a big deal, but that day was the day that I started my period! I panicked. I felt my face grow hot. Yes, I had a huge, super-long maxi pad in my purse!

If that wasn't enough mortification for the rest of my teenage years, the boy started to play catch with my maxi-pad with other boys in the class! I sat watching as they threw my most personal item all over the room. I tried and tried to get it away, but they just laughed louder and harder until I finally ran out of the room. I was sick. Here I was, the new girl, trying to make a good first impression, and this tragic event occurred. I convinced my mom to let me stay home sick the next day.

I was certain my life was ruined forever. As I think back on this experience now, I laugh out loud, but you can imagine the embarrassment I felt at that moment. The maxi-pad jokes continued for the next two years of junior high school. Right before my freshman year of high school, we moved to a city about 30 minutes away from where I grew up.

I was relieved to have a fresh start. But I was wiser; I now knew what *not* to carry in your purse. Lesson # 1: Don't keep your feminine products, especially really large ones, in a place where boys can get to them.

Starting over

I started high school ready to take on the world. I was not going to let a maxi-pad incident happen to me again! I wanted to be noticed, to be popular, to be cool. It didn't take long for the boys to start noticing me. I got asked to the junior prom my freshmen year, and that started a negative pattern-I was never "boy-friendless" again. I dated a boy for awhile, when it didn't work out we broke up, and I started dating another boy.

A boy named Patrick asked me to his junior prom. He became my first serious boyfriend. He was tall, dark, and handsome. He had a beautiful singing voice, and he liked me. That was the most important part about our relationship. I felt good when I was with him because he made me feel special. It wasn't so much about him, but about me. I enjoyed that he noticed me. He drove me to and from school everyday. We had the same friends so we went to the same parties. I found myself wanting to spend every waking moment with him no matter what it took to make that happen. I even started lying to my parents about where I was going and who I was going to be with. I think I spent most of my freshmen year grounded because they always caught me in a lie. Despite my parents' disapproval and discipline, my behavior didn't change. I continued to lie and find ways to see my boyfriend. My parents felt that he was a bad influence on me and wanted to limit the time we spent together. I didn't understand or appreciate their rules, so I continued to disobey them.

Big Mistake
One night Patrick called me and asked if he could come over. I told him that I was still grounded, but that didn't seem to bother him. We talked for awhile and decided that after my parents went to bed that I would sneak him up to my room.

Girl 2 girl chat:
Wait! Stop a minute! Did you catch what I said? Read it again. Sneak him up to my room? What was I thinking? First of all, did we really think my parents wouldn't notice? More importantly, I claimed to be a Christ follower. I knew inviting a boy into my bedroom was not the right move. But I didn't want

to sleep with him! We were just going to cuddle and talk. Those were *my* thoughts at least. We would play games, like Monopoly or Uno; I just wanted to be with him! Honestly, at that time, sex was far from my mind.

So, when my parents went to bed, I quietly snuck down the stairs and let my boyfriend in the backdoor. He said that he got in a fight with his dad and didn't have a place to go. I couldn't leave him out there. I had to let him in. My parents would understand…right?

Wrong! He got as far as my bedroom door when my mom knocked. "Uh-oh," I thought. "What do I tell her now?" The best idea that I could come up with was to hide him in my walk-in closet. "Surely, she won't look there," I prayed desperately. My heart was racing as I opened the door. "Oh, hi Mom," I managed nonchalantly.

"Angie, what are you doing up?" she asked.

"I was just talking on the phone," I lied.

"Really? Why where you downstairs?" she questioned. My mom knew the answers to all of her questions. I think she was just being kind and giving me the chance to tell her the truth. I never gave it to her. "Angie, who's in your closet?" she prompted.

"What are you talking about?" I said hoarsely. Duh! My mom walked right over to my closet and opened the door. My boyfriend stood there grinning sheepishly, shadowed by my jean dress. Did he think my mom couldn't see him? That's when my mom lost it! She icily told my boyfriend to get out of my closet and asked him to leave.

All my mom said to me the rest of the evening was, "What were you thinking?" What was I thinking? The next day I was grounded indefinitely.

Girl 2 girl chat:

Okay, so first off what WAS I thinking? From the beginning of my book all I've been talking about is how I wanted and desired attention. I wanted someone to notice me. Yeah. I did. I wanted someone to see me and say, "Wow, you are beautiful" or "You are so cute." Have you ever noticed that many girls want this same thing? All of us do. Why is that? Why do we want to be desired by someone? Why do we straighten or curl our hair? Why do we put makeup on? Why do we dress the way we do? Well, my answer was always "to impress the boys". Do you feel the same way? Are you out there doing your "thang" just to impress the boys? I think that's why I said yes to this tragic and stupid event. I couldn't say no to this cute boy who wanted to spend time with me, right?

Do you know what is so awesome about God? He noticed us even before we were born. He had His eye on us. He knows our every move, our every thought, our every disappointment, our every success. He notices us and loves us so much. Listen to these words found in Romans 8:39 "Neither height, nor depth, nor anything else in all creation, will be able to separate us from the love of God that is in Christ Jesus our Lord."

Wow! Nothing can separate us from His love. No matter how hard we try. He loves us regardless of our faults, regardless of our sins, regardless of our past, regardless of what we look like. He loves us and He notices us. In fact, listen to this in Psalm 139:13-16…this will rock your world, "For you created my inmost being; you knit me together in my mother's womb. I praise you because I am fearfully and wonderfully made; your works are wonderful, I know that full well. My frame was not hidden from you when I was made in the secret place. When I was woven together in the depths of the earth, your eyes saw my unformed body. All the days ordained for me were written in your book before one of them came to be."

What? God knew me before I was even born? How amazing is that? So, does He notice you? Yes, He loves you so much that He thought of you even before you came to be! Amazing! He also says in Isaiah 43: 4 "You are precious and honored in my sight, and because I love you."

So, now you're asking yourself, "Okay so what if this God loves me. I'm looking for love here on earth. It's nice to have someone take a second look at me, or admire me from across the hall. I want that kind of love and attention."

Mistake Number Two

You would think that this experience would have taught anyone with a brain an important lesson. Not me! I was a glutton for punishment. To answer your question, I don't really know what I was thinking. All I knew was this boy gave me attention. That was all that really mattered. I would do just about anything to not give up being noticed by him. I don't think I even thought of the "what ifs". I just wanted him to continue to like me, whatever it took. Well, needless to say I was banned from doing just about everything.

My friends started to wonder if I'd ever get to leave my house. One weekend both my parents had to go out of town. They decided to leave me in the care of my older brother. Considering his rebellious past, they would later regret their decision. Years before, my brother had a senior party at our house while my parents were out of town. The whole school showed up. People we didn't know steadily streamed through our doorway. There was alcohol, drugs, strangers having sex in my bedroom, girls dancing on our kitchen table, and more. It was the party of the century. My brother wouldn't have gotten caught, but my parents found the broken table parts that my brother tried to piece together. Oops! He was grounded for a long time. Thankfully, at that point, I was still considered an innocent bystander.

My parents must have forgotten about that incident or chose to forget because they left us home alone again for the weekend. I hadn't seen Patrick much since my mom found him in my closet, so I decided to invite him over one evening while my parents were gone. My brother was in his room listening to the radio with his headset on, so I snuck Patrick in my room. I locked the door. My brother never even knew that he was there. It was late and eventually my brother fell asleep. We talked, listened to the radio, danced, kissed, and then kissed some more. Before I knew it, he was getting into my bed. I liked him. I thought that I even loved him. He was wonderful. He liked me, was cute, and he treated me well. He made me feel special when I was with him. I was no longer the dorky girl from Christian school. I was popular and this gorgeous guy was noticing *me*.

We spent most of the night kissing and getting pretty intimate. We never had sex, as far as I was concerned. We just touched each other and kissed a lot. This was my first real experience with physical intimacy. At one point, we almost had sex, but then I shared with him that I wanted to wait until marriage. He seemed to understand. I was glad that he respected me and didn't push me to have sex with him.

Girl 2 girl chat:

He respected me? Funny now that I look back on the situation. If he respected me then don't you think that he wouldn't have done any of those things? If he respected me then he probably would have never even come over to my house when my parents weren't home.

So there I was, wanting a relationship so badly that I would do anything to keep him liking me. And besides, it felt good to kiss him. It felt good to be in his strong arms. He made me feel special.

Chapter Two

Being in Love

Being in love is an amazing thing. You act silly. You do crazy things. You just feel different. I was in love. This was the guy. I was convinced that he was the one. Mind you, I was only a freshmen in high school, but I knew love! (notice the sarcasm)

Then Patrick broke up with me. Heartbroken and misunderstood, I took the pieces of my heart and pleaded with him. What was wrong with me? Did I do something?

I never really got an answer. It was just over. Everything that we shared together was gone. It meant nothing to him. I struggled for several weeks thinking that I was not good enough. I would find ways to be around Patrick to "get his attention" again. I would purposely walk past his locker to see if his eyes would turn…nothing, not even a blink. He found himself another girl, and left me wondering what happened, and what was wrong with me. After my dramatic few months of mourning, I decided to get on with my life. Then I fell in love again. I fell hard this time. This time **he**'s the one!

Mr. Perfect

Remember the story at the beginning of the book about the boy in the library? Let me refresh your memory if you don't remember. His name was Gabe. He was a football player, popular, and handsome. He introduced himself to me in the library one day, and it was history from there.

It started with him asking me to go with him to a winter dance. It was a formal dance, and I of course said "yes". Great way to get dressed up, and look beautiful to win this boy's heart!

I could not wait for the night. I picked out the cutest dress and shoes to go with it. I wanted to wear my hair down so I curled every strand. My makeup matched perfectly to what I was wearing. I was ready for the best night of my life! I sat by the door anxiously waiting for Gabe to arrive. He pulled up in his black sports car, and I could hardly contain myself. He looked handsome in his double breasted black suit as he approached the door. After we said hello to one another my mom reminded us to put on our corsages. We made several attempts to put them on one another, but had no success. I was happy to have him close to me as he tried to not pin me or himself. He smelled really good, like one of those magazine ads for men's cologne…I couldn't get enough of that smell. My heart was pounding! I could tell that he was shaking a bit too. My mom had to save us from embarrassment, and she successfully pinned on our flowers. My dad took several photos. He probably went through an entire role of film. I think my parents were just glad that I wasn't with Patrick. They seemed to be impressed with Gabe. My brother called him the future president.

The date was more than I had ever dreamed it would be. The country club was decorated beautifully, the food was wonderful, and the company was sweet. Our conversation never stopped during dinner. He was not only adorable, but he was intelligent too! At one point he literally swept me off of my feet and asked me to dance. I really loved to dance but was not good at slow dancing. He was not the best dancer either, but he spun me around the dance floor like he knew what he was doing. My toes hurt due to being stepped on all night, but it didn't matter because we were having so much fun. It seemed like everyone was watching and smiling at us. We just seemed to click. We danced all night long. It was like a movie where all the other people froze in time, and it was just us. Alone, dancing and laughing. A song came on, and he started singing it to me while we danced. It was truly romantic. Was this guy for real? No one had ever swept me off of my feet like that! He sings too? Not the best singer, actually he was terrible, but the thought of it made my heart leap! Am I dreaming? This is only our first date…and it was absolutely….perfect.

Mr. Perfect & Me

Gabe was the most romantic guy I had ever met at the time. He'd give me roses every month for our anniversary. He would have them delivered to my class during the school day. If that wasn't enough to melt a girl's heart; he would also write me love letters, and slip them in my locker. He took me to fancy dinners almost every weekend. We went to all of the dances together. We took romantic walks by the river in the winter. We'd sit in front of his parent's fireplace sipping hot chocolate and talked about our future together. He treated me like a princess! All of my friends were jealous, and wished that their boyfriends acted like mine.

I was getting everything that I needed from Gabe, the love, affection, gifts and attention.

What more could a girl want? He was perfect.

I remember one Christmas he surprised me with a little jewelry box. I nervously opened it thinking that he was proposing. Inside was a beautiful diamond and pearl ring. I had never received such a gift and did not know how to respond. He did share with me that he wasn't proposing yet, but that one day he would. We began to plan our lives together.

Gabe was the one I would marry. I just felt it.

We had little in common. He was interested in politics, sports and graduating with honors. I enjoyed drama, choir, hanging out with my friends and just graduating.

These differences didn't bother either of us, we had an incredible relationship. They say that opposites attract anyway, right? So there we were, high school sweethearts. Anyone could see that we had a future together.

We did everything together. I liked my time with him. My parents didn't even seem to mind my time with him. I guess they recognized his potential. All they cared about was that this boyfriend wasn't getting me into trouble.

Is this a problem?
On occasion the subject would come up about religion, and we just didn't agree on things.

He was raised in a strict Catholic home; while I was raised in a Christian home.

Because of my beliefs, I told him at the beginning of our relationship that I would never have pre-marital sex. I didn't feel any pressure from him from the start, but I just felt like he needed to know. I didn't understand my reasons for it. I just remember in youth group my leader saying that it was "bad to have sex before marriage". I never really understood why exactly. I thought that it was mainly to keep us from getting pregnant young. I didn't see any other real reason why not. But I vowed to keep myself pure anyway. He seemed like he understood, so we just had a great time being boyfriend and girlfriend going out on dates.

Being together seemed like it was enough. We enjoyed each other's company, we talked, we had fun joking around. We even joked about the whole "sex" issue. I remember one weekend we were just going for a drive, and we found a couple that had "parked" nearby.

We started yelling at them out our window. They must have thought that we were the park patrol or something, because they sped off quickly. We followed them around just to freak them out! I bet they never "parked" again!

Gabe and I dated all throughout high school from our sophomore year on.

Aside from the thought that he and I didn't share in the same "religion", I felt that he was the perfect match for me.

But, we were destined for failure because of my lack of concern in this matter. In all honesty, something just didn't feel right. I continued to disregard those feelings though because of my happiness with him. I mean, why does religion really matter? Yes, I have a relationship with Jesus Christ, and I believe all of that. But why does it matter what my boyfriend believes? I don't know. All I know is that love blinds you. It forces you to not think about reality sometimes.

Girl 2 girl chat:

So this is a good question. Are you in a relationship where your boyfriend does not believe the same things as you? Is this really a problem? I didn't think that it was. We'll chat more about that issue later.

Too Close for Comfort

I also disregarded many other things. Gabe and I started becoming intimately involved. It didn't happen all at once. It was a gradual thing. One kiss here, another there.

Before I knew it, he was asking me to sleep over at his parent's house while they were out of town. Let me explain something before I go on. In my eyes then, we weren't having sex…that is the act of intercourse. We did everything else that we could, but we were NOT having sex!

Girl 2 girl chat:

I really believed this. I believed that since we were just having a little fun touching each other and kissing on each other that we were NOT having sex. I mean when I was taught in junior high school what sex was it was all about the putting, "the you know what inside the you know what". No one ever told me that sex also means other things. Once again, I didn't understand until later, that even though it wasn't the act of intercourse, I was still involving myself in sex. Throughout all of this something just didn't feel right. Something was tugging at my heart screaming for me to end the relationship, but I was completely ignoring the voice. I felt loved, wanted, beautiful, sexy, and I was not letting this go.

The sin

After the intimacy increased, our dates always ended up in his bedroom. No more great talks by the fireplace. No more feelings of a future. It was all sexual from that point on. We argued more than we ever had, and things just weren't the same. What happened to our relationship? We were so close. We'd have such wonderful conversations…what happened to all of that? I did break it off a couple of times but

Finding My Pure Heart Again

I would always run back to him when he'd ask for a 2nd chance. How could I not? He was adorable, and he seemed to really like me. He even told me that he loved me!

It was the summer before our senior year. His brother who was in college asked us if we wanted to watch his apartment while he was away. Thinking back, why did his apartment need "to be watched"? I mean come on! But there I was again, I desired to be with SOMEONE. I wanted to be loved, to be noticed. So I agreed to the apartment watching. At this point I got really good at lying to my parents. As far as they knew, I was staying with a girl friend of mine for the weekend. I planned the whole weekend out. I brought over movies, games, and Chinese food. I wanted to get close to him again, to get our old relationship back, to put aside our differences, and really discover who each other was.

It wasn't long after dinner that we started getting intimate. I guess no scrabble tonight! We kissed and from there got more intimate than we had ever gotten before. Don't get me wrong, it felt nice. I was enjoying it. We had almost had "real" sex, when he stopped to say that he didn't have a condom. The only thing that ran through my mind was "thank you God"! I didn't have enough conviction on my own to stop so God intervened for me...well, almost.

Gabe proceeded to tell me that the drug store was just around the corner. There blows the thought of God helping me out! We left the apartment, and walked down the cold hall to where the parking garage was. As we walked, I just knew that this is not the choice I really wanted to make. I knew that what we were about to do was wrong. Yes, we loved each other, but why did we have to rush into this. Why now? I walked quietly to the car as he, the gentlemen that he was, opened the door for me. I sat down in his clean sports car and suddenly felt so alone. What was I doing here? Gabe got in the car, and we drove in silence only a few blocks away. I waited in the car as he bought his first condom. He looked proud of himself as he walked through the aisles. My mind raced. What was I doing? I felt so used, so dirty, so un-loved.

I know now that God was helping me out…He was giving me those feelings of something not being right. He was convicting my heart, encouraging me to say "no". I think He even had the interruptions happen to give me a chance to get out of the situation. But He wanted me to make the choice. He wanted me to stand up to how I felt about sex. Wasn't it intended for marriage? My thoughts were interrupted by Gabe's peeling out of the store's parking lot. I didn't know what to say. Why wouldn't I speak up? I mean this boy loved me. We'll probably be married one day. So, what's the problem? There is no problem, I convinced myself. We will get married one day. We've talked about it before. So everything is okay.

By the time we got back to the apartment I had changed my tune. I did not want Gabe to get mad at me, break up with me, or think I was a prude, so I walked back into the bedroom with him. We started all over again, and all the while my heart was weeping. Gabe politely asked me if I still wanted to.

Wanted to? Whoever said I ever really wanted to? It just happened! Well, even though this could have been my 3rd out, I said, "I guess so, we've come this far already."

<u>Girl 2 girl chat</u>:
   Come this far? What was I thinking? Just because we've come this far, I'd agree to have sex with him? I could have spoken up. I could have said "no". I could have told him that I just didn't feel comfortable with doing this. But I didn't. I froze. I just wanted his love. That's all. And I believed that by doing this with him, I'd win his heart forever.

   About a half hour later, tears flowed from my eyes. He asked me what was wrong...I told him that I loved him.
   The funny thing, that wasn't the reason why I was crying. I was crying because I gave into something that was supposed to be so special, so perfect, so intended for marriage. It was too late. I had lost my virginity. That quickly it was gone.
   I was speechless, but a million things ran through my head.
   Did that just really happen?
   I just turned 17. This is my senior year.
   I'm not even out of school yet.
   I'm not a virgin anymore.
   I'm not a virgin anymore.
   I'm not a virgin anymore.
   What was I thinking?

Girl 2 girl chat:

1 Thess. 5:6 "…let us be alert and self-controlled." 4: 7 " God did not call us to be impure, but to live a holy life." 5: 8 "…be self-controlled" I Corin. 6: 19-20"…flee from sexual immorality, all other sins a man commits are outside his body, but he who sins sexually sins against his own body. Do you not know that your body is a temple of the Holy Spirit, who is in you, whom you have received from God? You are not your own, you were bought at a price. Therefore honor God with your body."

I know now that this was not honoring God with my body. God intended sex for marriage. He wanted me to wait until I committed myself to someone. Let me re-phrase that "some ONE". Meaning only one person, I did not commit myself to Gabe in marriage. I didn't really even know if we'd really get married one day. But the point is that until we actually got married, we had no right exploring into intimacy like we did. There's a chapter later on talking more specifically about how having sex before you're married will affect you. And let me tell you…it does affect you.

Chapter Three

Relationship Broken

I didn't tell anyone about what happened. My best friend didn't even know. I was too completely ashamed. What would she think of me? What would anyone think of me for that matter? I wanted to just pretend like it didn't happen, except it happened almost every weekend. We were having sex on a regular basis, and I was continuously giving in to it. I'm not blaming this boy. I know that I had a mouth to speak, and chose my own paths.

Why didn't I tell him that I didn't feel right doing it? He didn't have a clue that this was bothering me. How could he know? I never told him. Each night that we went out we would end up on the floor at his parent's house under blankets in case they walked in.

Why did his parents have such trust in us? Maybe they just didn't want to know what was going on in their basement. Who knows? All I know is that our relationship was changing. It was not getting better. It was taking a turn for the worst. We barely talked. We didn't do much of anything for that matter. We just had sex.

I was starting to think that Gabe stopped caring about me. Everything had changed. I wasn't being swept off of my feet anymore by him. He didn't captivate me anymore. No more notes in my locker. No more flowers. We fought about everything.

We would always make up, of course. Make up then we'd make out. Then we'd have sex.

I know what most of you are thinking. Why didn't I break up with him? I don't know to tell you the truth. I guess I didn't like the thought of being "alone". I wanted to have a place to go, someone to talk to at night on the phone, someone to hold my hand down the hall, someone to send me flower. You get the point. Even though all of these things stopped, I still desired them and longed for that kind of love and attention. Most importantly I wanted someone to make me feel special. I didn't feel special before, and when I was with someone I WAS special. I was finally, after all these years, being noticed.

God Noticed Me

<u>Girl 2 girl chat:</u>
I had always gone to church with my family every Sunday morning and Wednesday night for youth group. I knew the lingo, I knew the scriptures, the stories, and I certainly knew how, and how not to act. One thing I never really knew or understood was

how much God truly loved me. I heard about it, sang about, and I even talked about it. But I never really knew in my heart how special I was to him. The meaning of the scripture, " I am fearfully and wonderfully made," was not understood until I reached the age of 30. Since I was young, I longed to be loved and to be told that I was beautiful. I dreamed of being rescued from my castle tower by a handsome, strong prince. Hasn't every little girl felt this way? My daughter is the perfect example of a little girl who longs to be admired. When she was four years old she would dance around the room in her little princess outfit desiring her daddy's admiration and longing for a slow dance with the only man in her life. It was precious to see her face as he lifted her in his arms. Her smile lit up and she had a loving look in her eyes. It's like she was saying, "He's noticed me, I am special."

Stacie Eldredge explains this in her book Captivating…"and finally every woman wants to have a beauty to unveil. Not to conjure, but to unveil. Most woman feel the pressure to be beautiful from very young, but that is not what I speak of. There is also a deep desire to simply and truly be the beauty, and be delighted in." Eldredge continues, " No one is fighting for her heart; there is no grand adventure to be swept up in; and every woman doubts very much that she has any beauty to unveil."

Unfortunately the world's view of beauty is very different from the way God had intended it to be. The world tells us to dress immodestly, to have "perfect" figures, "pearly" white teeth, slim strong bodies, flawless skin...no imperfections allowed at all! When you think about it, this is an unattainable goal! If we do everything that the world is telling us to do then we'd all be fake! Fake but at least beautiful!

God tells us in 1 Samuel 16:7, "The Lord does not look at the things man looks at. Man looks at the outward appearance, but the Lord looks at the heart." Then in 1 Peter 3:3, "Your beauty should not come from outward adornment, such as braided hair and the wearing of gold jewelry and fine clothes. Instead, it should be that of your inner self, the unfading beauty of a gentle and quiet spirit, which is of great worth in God's sight." God doesn't see your pimples or your handicap, if you talk funny or look different from everyone else. In fact, He is the one that created you. He made you perfect in His sight! He doesn't look at your outward appearance. God sees your heart.

So, there I was for many years in my life trying to be something I really wasn't. I wanted to be beautiful, to be perfect, to fit in, and to be noticed. God had already made me perfect...in His eyes...I just needed to figure that out myself...the hard way.

Living a lie

I continued to go to youth group. I continued to date Gabe. I continued to pretend that we were not having sex. I continued to pretend I was happy. No one knew. I feared getting a bad reputation so I asked Gabe to swear that he wouldn't tell anyone. Back then people called you a slut for sleeping with someone. Today teens are bragging about how many people they've had sex with. I just didn't want anyone to know because I felt guilty. There were people in my school that knew I was a Christian, and up until this point knew that I was different from everyone else, because I didn't drink, or smoke, or swear. I didn't want people to know, because I knew that it was wrong.

We continued our relationship through our senior year like this. As the year was closing out on us something happened. I'm not sure what exactly, but something happened. I was fed up. I was tired of living a lie, and I wanted to stop the relationship for good. I took the ring that he gave me and made up some lame excuse about why I was breaking it off. Still never revealing the truth why I actually broke up with him. It might have done him some good to know that sex ruined our relationship, but I never told him.

Girl 2 girl chat

Romans 7:15; 8:5, "I do not understand what I do. For what I want to do I do not do, but what I hate I do. And if I do what I do not want to do, I agree that the law is good. As it is, it is no longer I myself who do it, but it is sin living in me." This verse is about Paul who pretty much admits that he sins everyday. He says that he is constantly doing things that he really does not want to do, but he keeps on doing them. This is exactly what I was doing in this relationship. I knew that it wasn't right, but I kept on doing it. Read the verses again. It gets confusing sometimes, but it also makes so much sense.

Picking up the pieces

I swore that I would not get involved with someone the remainder of the year. My senior year was almost up, and I needed to focus on graduating. My friends kept me busy with things because they knew how difficult it was for me to finally break up with Gabe. I enjoyed not having a boyfriend. My whole high school career, up until then, someone had been with me. This was the first time I had been "single" in a long time.

I had a close guy friend whom I had confided in a lot, and we began to hang out more and more. I told him to not get any ideas because I was not dating anyone. He laughed then, but over the next couple of weeks began to lure me in. He was my good friend, and we hung out. He knew how I felt about guys at this point yet still charmed and romanced me. I was strong for several weeks then finally gave in. Why not? He's harmless. We shared in the same beliefs about things, and he went to my youth group. How could this go wrong? We'll just go out together to have fun. He also knew how I felt about intimacy because we talked about it at our youth group. Surely, we would never go over board. Right?

I thought that I was picking up the pieces here. What happened to being single for the rest of the year? This friend and I dated and soon we were intimately involved. I did have the guts to tell him that we were not going to have intercourse. So we just did everything else under the sun! I was not going to make that mistake twice. I guess I should have seen this pattern unfolding again. The more we got intimate the less we talked. Soon our relationship failed and we no longer were friends. I stood alone again, with my broken heart.

Girl 2 girl chat
I just have to say it again....I think so many young people struggle with the same lie. I really believed that the act of intercourse was "having sex," so I was perfectly okay with doing all of the "other stuff." "I'm not having SEX" I'd convince myself. But I was. I was giving my body to someone before I was married...this is sex.

The First Stephen
After I graduated from high school I decided to take a semester off before going to college. I needed some time to get my head clear. I worked, slept in late, and enjoyed the free time that I had. My best friend wanted me to go out with her and her boyfriend one night. The catch? They were bringing along another friend...Stephen. Oh, okay, I guess I'll go out with him, just this once... as a favor. I did not want to get involved again. But we went out and had a great time. Then we went out again...and again...and again. Then we started getting intimate. Are you seeing a pattern here? I didn't even really like this guy. He was cute, but that was about all. I didn't have feelings for him. So, why was I kissing him? Why was I letting him touch me?

...and the other Stephen

At the same time that I was seeing Stephen, another Stephen came into the picture. A friend from high school told me that he was interested in me and wanted to ask me out. He graduated a couple years before me but always had a crush on me. To tell you the truth, I didn't even know him in high school. But he seemed charming so I thought I'd just get to know him. He invited me to dinner at his house one night. He knew that I loved pasta, so he made me an incredible Italian dinner. We got dressed up, had dinner by candlelight, and then we just sat and talked. He was adorable. He was a little quirky in ways, but charming. To my surprise, nothing else happened that night. We just had fun.

I continued to date both Stephens. Not on the same day of course, but one date with one, another date with the other. It was absolutely crazy! My friends made fun of me..."Which Stephen are you going out with tonight?" they'd say. Whatever happened to getting my head clear anyway? I didn't have time for anything because I was constantly entertaining some guy. Well it turned out that the first Stephen was only wanting a good make out session, so I broke it off with him. But the second Stephen was falling quickly for me. He'd write me poems. He'd leave me gifts on my car before I went to work. He was a gentlemen. He would have been a good catch if I wasn't so screwed up. I didn't want to hurt this guy, so I told him that I needed some time alone. I explained to him that I had just gotten out of a relationship and that I didn't think I was ready for anything serious

Finding My Pure Heart Again

again. He kindly understood. He was very sweet. He wrote me one more "goodbye" poem and went on his way. Finally, I was free again!

Wrong! Guess who showed up at my doorstep one afternoon? Gabe, my high school sweetheart. He said that he was in the area and wanted to see how I was doing. Sounds fishy to me! How did he know that I wasn't dating anyone anyway? Do these guys know each other? Do they get together and say, "Okay, she's available again"?

Well, to make a long story short. He was back in the picture again. He seemed like he had really changed. He seemed more mature. More aware of how things went wrong between us. He said that he would do anything to have me back in his life again. Wow! That is quite a statement. Anything? He'd do anything for me? This was my chance. Tell him that if you get involved again that you refuse to get intimate!

Tell him!

Tell him!

Opportunity number four. Gone. I never told him.

We were in the same mess that we were in during high school.

Only this time we had more free time alone together.

I remember one night we walked to a park. It was dark. We had our blankets in hand and we were going to star gaze among nature. We ended up being a part of nature. We layed there naked in the middle of nowhere having sex, because there was no where else for us to go. I remember thinking, "I'm not even hiding this anymore…I'm out here in the middle of a park where anyone could see us. I'm not even bothered…who cares anymore." I felt like it was too late. I was starting to push my guilty convictions aside.

Nothing seemed to work anyway. I'd continue to end up in a relationship like this no matter what I did. So I gave in to it once again, this time with no regrets.

But God wasn't finished with me yet. He kept pulling at my heart. I tried to ignore the feelings of guilt and being unsatisfied, but He wouldn't let me.

Girl 2 girl chat

Unsatisfied is an understatement. I was so used up; desperately wanting love and attention that I was willing to give myself completely to someone…again. Even after knowing full well that it wouldn't fulfill my needs. That same desire of wanting to be loved, to be noticed was driving me to accept these invitations so willingly. I forgot that God already loved me. That God already noticed me, and that He loved me so much He died for me. Okay that's great and all, but I wanted love here, on earth. To be held, to be told how beautiful I was. By the way this is completely normal, and we all want that. I just didn't know what to do with those desires. So I continued again and again to allow these broken relationships into my life so that I could feel temporarily satisfied.

Chapter Four

Alone with God

It happened one night. When I was least expecting it. I guess the feelings of guilt were haunting me. I sat alone in my room. Normally I would have had music on, but not this night. This night was different. I was totally fed up. I wanted my life to take a turn. I wanted what was right. I wanted out of the relationship. I fell to the ground pleading with God. "Please take this from me, I know this is not from you. I desire to have a Godly man in my life!" That was all that I said. That was all He wanted me to say. I cried for awhile then fell asleep.

Perfect time to Ponder

Gabe and his parents were on their way to England for the rest of the summer. I knew that this would give me a chance to think about how to approach the final breakup with him. He wrote me every week while he was gone and said that he desired to take our relationship a step further. How much further could we go? I'm still not sure what that meant. I do know that we were not going any further as a couple together. I was ending it for good! I spent a lot of my time without him just pondering the reasons for my behavior. Why and how did I get myself into this relationship? Was I searching for a prince to rescue me? Or was he just someone that paid really good attention to me and made me feel special? Either way, it had gone downhill. I wondered what could have been of our relationship had we not ventured into intimacy. Did we mess up a future together when we had sex? Maybe he was the one! What did we do?

God quickly reminded me of our differences and assured me that this was not a Godly relationship. Would I ever find one now, especially with what I had been thru and had already done? I didn't think I was deserving of a Godly man. But that is what I longed for. I longed for someone who would point me in the right direction. I wanted someone who would love me for who I am not for what I could offer him. I desired someone who sought out God for answers. I needed someone who believed the same things that I believed and lived it out. Was there someone out there like this for me? I believed that there had to be but I did not think that I was deserving of such a person. Why would God grant me such a blessing when I had done such wrong?

Weeks had passed and my decision was made. I may never find this true Godly love or deserve it, but I was definitely going to get out of the un-godly relationship that I was so deep into.

A Glimpse Into a Godly Man's Heart

It was the night of my graduation from my youth group at church. The leader had planned a party for all of us who were finally moving on. We sat together crying as a slide show of pictures displayed the past four years of our lives together. So many memories and treasured times with friends. As I sat watching the show I felt a sense of guilt. These were my closest friends. The friends I spent all of my time with sled riding, playing silly games, laughing, going on mission trips to other countries. These were my Christian brothers and sisters who did not know a thing about me. They knew the fun, goofy me, but not the me that struggled so much with so many issues. I would not let them in. I couldn't let them in. I did not want them to know the ugly side of me. In their eyes I was sweet, little innocent Angie. I didn't want to ruin their impression of me. But weren't these the friends that I was supposed to share my heart with? I needed their prayers and support, but instead of sharing with them I pretended like everything was fine.

At the end of the slide show as we all wiped the tears from our eyes, I passed around a journal book that I wanted everyone to sign. For some it was a simple, "Hey, thanks for the fun times," for others, "You're a great girl, keep shining for God"...keep shining for God? Did I play a role so beautifully that they really thought that I was shining for God? How sad it made me feel to think that I was looked up to; that people wanted their lives to "shine for God" like I did. If only I truly had. Can you imagine the real impact I would have had on people's lives? It could have been endless what God could have done in my life during high school if I would have let Him.

As the evening was ending I searched for my journal to take it home. I glanced over at a friend of mine whom I had known since I was in 2nd grade. David. He was three years older than me. He helped the youth pastor throughout the year doing the bible studies or just taking us to events. I had always looked up to David. He was a handsome, intelligent Godly man. The Godly man that I so longed for. While everyone had gotten up from their seats, David was still busy writing in my book. What in the world was he so intently writing? I was curious. He looked like he was starting to struggle with what to say. I walked over to him and asked if he was finished. He smiled and asked if he could take the book home to finish. He assured me that he would bring the book to my home when he had completed his work of art. Shocked and bewildered I agreed and went along my way.

Days later I was at home just relaxing when I received a phone call from one of the Stephens. He knew that I loved movies and wanted to know if I would watch one with him. I gave in, but told him that he had to come to my house. My parents were home, and I was not putting myself in another bad situation. Stephen brought the movie over, my mom made us spaghetti, and we watched it together…all three of us. It was quite funny to see his face when my mom wouldn't leave. I think he had other intentions for the afternoon.

A knock at the door made my mom finally get up to leave the room. I think Stephen felt a sigh of relief

Finding My Pure Heart Again

until she called me in to tell me that someone was there for me. My mom whispered, "It's David!".

Now let me go back a ways and explain something. David and I had gone to Christian school together since we were both young. He was best friends with my older brother and would always come over to hang out. I had always thought that he was a wonderful man. I even had a crush on him when we were little. He would always yell at my brother and stick up for me when my brother would shoe me out of his room. He was always kind to me and treated me with such gentleness. We had remained friends throughout school even though we were in different schools. When he went off to college he wrote to me on occasion. He was a good friend to have.

My mom had looked at things a little differently than me. She had always told me, since I was young, that one day I would marry David. I told her that she was crazy. Where would she get a thought like that? He could have any girl around. Why would he want me, especially if he knew my past?

So there I was sitting with Stephen when my mom called me in. She was smiling quite big. I opened the back door and there stood David with my journal in his hands. I stared in disbelief because he took the time to drive 30 minutes out of his day to bring me back my book. I thanked him and invited him in. He hesitated at first because of the other car in the driveway. Then my mom yelled out to him, "Come in David, have some spaghetti". It was an offer he couldn't refuse. He walked in, and we talked for a

Finding My Pure Heart Again

couple of minutes before I remembered that Stephen was sitting in the next room. Oops!

I introduced David to Stephen, and we all sat in the living room together eating pasta watching a silly cartoon. How awkward! I watched the clock slowly tick by as I tried to keep the tension light. I didn't know what to do. My mom just sat smiling watching me squirm. Finally the movie was over and David thanked my mom for the warm invitation. It was nice to have him there. Even though we all felt strangely out of place he still seemed grateful. I walked him to the door and said goodbye.

My mom and I quickly ran into the other room and read the page that David had written in my book. He knew that I loved palm trees so he drew me a beautiful beach setting with a palm tree on one side of the page. The other page read, " There are few people that posess the qualities that you have in such abundance. Your smile is so soothing, your eyes display such a gentle spirit, and your heart is filled with much passion and tenderness. You are a joy to be around and a blessing to have as a friend. We have so many memories…karate classes together, piano, songs, youth group, retreats (well some retreats, sorry definitely a very large mistake) anyway, follow your passions…with love, David."

How sweet! How unfortunate that I fooled him too. I was about to start feeling the guilt again when my mom interrupted my thoughts with, " He is obviously sorry that things didn't work out for you two." What? Where did she get that from the letter? I read it again.

Let's go back about 2 years prior. In between boyfriends, David had asked me to go with him to a concert. I truly did not feel like this was a "date" because it was with David, my friend, someone that I had known my whole life practically. Of course my mom had other thoughts. In her eyes she had been right about David all of these years. It was finally happening. Our relationship was budding! He would swoon me then he would marry me! "Calm down, mom. We are just friends." I insisted. In the back of my mind (actually it was pretty close to the front of my mind) I had hoped that she was right. He was adorable.

We went to the concert, had an amazing time and on occasion we'd see a movie or just hung out together. Nothing romantic really came about it, but I could tell that sparks were starting to fly now. He had never looked at me like the way that he did then.

A couple months passed and our youth group planned a trip to a retreat about an hour away. We were all going. David included. When we arrived there were other youth groups from the area on the same retreat. David started hanging out with an old "friend" and I was pretty much not talked to the rest of the weekend. She was beautiful, tall, with long black hair. I was hurt but I never said anything about it. I treasured our friendship. I didn't want anything to come in between that. Besides, she seemed more like his type. So, I let it go, and we never mentioned what happened. We remained friends, and at that time that was much more important to me.

Okay then! I was getting what my mom was talking about. He felt bad for what had happened on that retreat and this was his way of telling me that he was sorry. It was sweet. But I guess I didn't look at it further. Of course, my mom's eyes began to sparkle again. To tell you the truth, it made me glad that he was trying to make amends, but I didn't want to get him involved in a very complicated person such as myself. He was deserving of a Godly woman, who could give him her all. I didn't have much more to give. So I just brushed it off as David being himself.

One Starry Night
Several weeks later my best friend, Margaret invited me to her house one night after a get together at our church. She said that other friends of ours were coming to just hang out. She had to take her cousin to the airport first, so she told me to be there in about one hour. I got there and the house was dark. They had not gotten back yet. So I just sat in my car and listened to the radio. It was a beautiful, warm summer night, and I enjoyed the peace of being alone. I quietly prayed. "Lord, I really want Your help here. How do I end this relationship with Gabe…for good this time? Is there any hope for me? Will I ever find a Godly man?" I sat in my car for about a half hour before the lights from another car blinded my sight. I had no idea which of our friends this was. It may even be my best friend coming home from the airport. I waited until I recognized the driver of the vehicle who pulled up next to me in the driveway. A smile I recognized. David.

"Okay God, not funny! I know that David is a Godly man, but he would never be for me.

I'll love him as my friend, my brother in Christ, like you have called me to do."

Really, what were the chances? I smiled as David got out of his car and knocked on my window. I invited him to sit with me on the roof of my car to star gaze.

The sky was so clear it seemed like you could see every star. We joked about how neither of us knew anything about astronomy but pretended like we did. It was glorious to just sit and gaze upon God's beauty. To think that He strategically placed each star in the sky, it was beyond words. David and I sat for it seemed like hours on the hard roof of my car just laughing and talking, when he shocked me with a simple question.

"Do you even know what happened a couple of years ago?"

I must have looked confused because he continued, "Would you like to know?" Another dumb founded look.

"I was crazy about you Angie. I thought things were happening between us. When we got to that retreat, I froze. I kept thinking that you were my best friend's little sister. And I didn't know what to do with that. Your brother never said anything to me about it, but it seemed like the wrong time. So I just stopped. I should have told you."

Crazy about me? Me? Is he kidding? I was floored! I didn't know how to respond but I blurted out," You were crazy about me? I was crazy about you. I just didn't want to mess up our friendship so I let it go."

We sat and talked for awhile longer when my best friend and her boyfriend arrived. I think David and I were both glowing because they kept asking what was going on. I couldn't put it into words. I just kept smiling.

No one else showed up so the four of us decided to go up to the local beach and sit and star gaze some more. While our friends walked along the beach David and I continued our conversation. We were both shocked that we were having the same feelings. Then a cop came and urged us to find somewhere else to go since it was curfew.

We called it a night and David and I agreed that we would continue our talk the next day. I drove home, confused, yet enlightened and dreamy eyed. What was God doing? Did He have his hand on this? I just asked him for a Godly man in my life only a couple of days ago. I truly wasn't looking for one right now, I just meant eventually. I didn't want to jump the gun, so I retreated in my thoughts and decided it was best to just sleep on it and find out what David had to say in the morning.

Girl 2 girl chat

This idea of getting into another relationship really scared me. I truly did not want to mess things up with David as my friend. Yet there was something drawing me to him. I just wanted God's hand in this. If this was to bud into a relationship I wanted to seek God first. Otherwise, I would continue on with a pattern that I didn't want in my life. And I certainly did not want to hurt David in any way. I wanted my focus to be on the lover of my soul and I wanted Him to fill those voids in my life, not an earthly man.

Chapter Five

Answered Prayer

The night that I pleaded with God was finally the last draw for me, I wanted what God wanted. He wanted me to be faithful to him, to concentrate on him, to look to him for answers. David and I spent time together over the next couple of days talking about a relationship. He wanted to be with me and told me that he had for quite some time now. I was in awe. I had no idea. We were such good friends that I never saw a relationship coming again with him. He said that he could never get a chance to tell me how he felt because I was always dating someone else. Here I was longing for a Godly relationship, and it was right in front of my eyes. I was so blinded by the first guy that gave me attention, and I wasn't really thinking about what God wanted for me.

I wanted this to be different. It was David, I couldn't let it go sour. It would mess up things for both of us. I especially didn't want him to get hurt.

I was a little hesitant at first, but I knew that deep down, my heart was always with David. I jokingly told him that he was about three years late on getting together with me. If only we were together earlier in life. Things may have been different. But I know that God's timing is perfect, and there was a reason for all of this. The reason, I wouldn't find out for years to come.

Climbing upward

I loved the idea that David and I shared in the same passion of our relationship with Christ. Because of this, we attended church together, and had weekly bible studies. Here was the man that I once had a crush on years prior. I looked up to him spiritually. I dreamed that my mom was right about her "feelings" that one day we would get together, but never really thought that it would happen. And here he was in my life again.

He loved God, and that was what I'd longed for.

What a different relationship than the last. I am now climbing upward, looking to God for guidance in this relationship. Oh how I longed for cleanliness. I wanted our relationship to remain pure, and never step over the boundaries God has set out for us.

David and I had such fun together. Since we'd known each other for so many years we didn't have to go through that unknown mystery of interests. We already knew each other's likes and dislikes. We enjoyed the same movies, food, television shows. We had the same friends. It made dating so much easier. We were like best friends just hanging out together.

The Return of the boyfriend in England

The time came when Gabe, who had been in England throughout the summer returned home. I knew that I would have to face him sometime. He called me the second he got in from the airport. "I want to see you. I've missed you so much. Could I stop by? I have something for you." "Yes, there are things I'd like to talk with you about" I nervously replied. I think he recognized the nervousness in my voice and asked if everything was okay. I told him that we'd talk when he got to my house. I immediately called David to ask him to pray for me. I wanted to be kind, yet I wanted to be strong. Gabe needed to know about David and what had happened between us while he was away.

Gabe arrived at my home, and he embraced me. I felt so strange. So much had occurred over the last few months. How would I explain this to him? I know that he said that he wanted things to go further for us, but my heart was saying "no". Not only was David in my life now, but I felt like God was pulling at my heart strings encouraging me to finally get out of this bad relationship for good. I sat him down after his long embrace, and he immediately sensed the tension. "What's going on? Did things change between us?" he asked.

I swallowed hard and said, "Yes, I'm sorry."

"What? Angie! How could this happen? Why didn't you tell me in your letters?" he gently asked.

"I didn't want your trip to be ruined, and things happened so fast." I replied, not really knowing how to respond.

He didn't look me in the eyes for several minutes. He was truly disappointed. Normally I would have taken everything back. I would have told him that we'd give it one more try. Not this time. It was over. Our relationship had to come to an end. He finally looked up at me and asked," It's David, isn't it?" My mouth dropped. What? How could he have known? I'd never mentioned anything about David to him. He only met him a couple of times at youth group. How would he know? It was almost like God was whispering hints in his ear, telling him to let go.

"Yes, it is David. I honestly did not see this coming." I said.

After we talked for awhile longer he finally gave in to the thought. He knew at that point I would not go back with him. It was over. "I still want you to have something." he said as he handed me a small box. I opened the box which held a necklace with a cross on it. It was beautiful.

"I can't take this." I said.

"Angie, you have to. When I saw it I thought of you. Please, you can remember me by it." he replied as he looked as though he would cry.

I took the necklace and thanked him. "I'm glad it's David. I know that he will take care of you." he said as he hugged me goodbye.

That was that. He kissed me on the cheek and went on his way. If I had known it was going to be that easy, I would have broken it off sooner. Then again, God's timing is perfect. His hand was in it this time. He knew that I submitted myself to Him, and that is why it went so smoothly.

Let the games begin

Not again… it didn't take long for David and I to start kissing. We had incredible feelings for one another it was bound to happen, right? It was always innocent and wonderful, but the more time we spent alone together, more sparks would fly. The longer our kisses got. The more intimate they felt. We were heading down the wrong path. I didn't realize until later that you have to be careful about spending time alone with someone you really care about. It almost always ends up bad. You hug a little, kiss a little, then before you know it you're having sex. I didn't want this to happen in our relationship. I'd been there, done that. Physical intimacy, outside of marriage, make things better, it only makes them worse. Besides, this was the godly man that I was waiting for. I didn't want to mess things up, but we kept kissing.

Girl 2 girl chat

What was with me? I had a voice. Why couldn't I speak up? Why couldn't I tell him that I thought this might not be a good idea?

I would always convince myself that nothing was wrong. We were just kissing. What harm is that? We liked each other. That's what couples do…they kiss. So, once again, I let things go on. We weren't doing anything wrong. The only thing I was doing wrong was not sharing my heart with David. I valued our relationship so you'd think that

I would fight to keep this one in tact. I remained silent. In my head the thoughts kept coming, "you're only kissing". Months later the kissing turned into heavy kissing, then weeks after that the heavy kissing turned into heavy touching.

And the pattern continued. We never had "sex", but again, wasn't this still considered "sex".

What were we thinking? Here we were two people that longed for the same things, yet gave in to the temptation so easily.

We continued this for several months. Every moment alone we had together turned physically intimate. I felt like the relationship was falling apart. I knew that eventually it would. I did not want that to happen.

A mother's intuition

I don't know if my mom ever knew what was going on between David and I, but I suspect that she did. One night she came up to my room and handed me a book on intimacy and marriage, and gently prompted me to read it. Now maybe she was just being mom, and this was her way of telling me the "birds and the bees", but I believe that God spoke to her to give me this book. At first, I was embarrassed. "Please mom!" I blushed.

If only she knew what I had already been through. I certainly did not need a lesson on how to get intimate. I was a pro at this point. I put the book aside knowing that I would probably never pick it up.

But the book kept screaming my name. I would see it sitting across the room hiding under some old fashion magazines, and my gaze would always be drawn back to it. So I finally picked it up and began to read. I read it through in one night. It spoke to me. It talked about the importance of being pure before your future husband. Pure, are you kidding? This was something I hadn't been in a long time. How could I be pure for my future husband? It was too late for me. I shouldn't even be allowed to wear white to my wedding. But I continued reading. Tears were endless that night.

When I finished the book, God spoke to my heart. I had to share with David what had happened to me in the past. I never told him because I was afraid it would change things for us. But more importantly, if I didn't tell him, I was afraid that we were headed down that same path. How could I tell him? Certainly he would want someone untouched and unblemished. What will he think of me? This is the man who has known me for years and has thought of me as an innocent princess. God kept whispering to the depth of my soul that this was His way. Purity was the only way to make a relationship truly alive in Him. My way was not working. My way brought about heartache and pain. My way ended in brokenness every time. I had to tell David no matter what the cost or our relationship would also end up as a bad memory.

That very night I prayed that God would give me the courage to tell him the truth. If he chose to leave me because of it, then I would have to deal with that. But I knew that he had the right to know.

David and I spent the next day together hanging out. I knew that I wanted to share with him what God was doing in my heart. "I want to talk with you about something David." I said as my voice shook.

"What is it? Is everything okay?" he asked.

"I've needed to tell you something for a long time and haven't gotten up the courage to do it until now. I just know that I have to do this." I said.

I hesitated for a brief moment then went on to tell him my story of losing my virginity and about the intimacy with my past boyfriends. It took him awhile to gather his thoughts. He was speechless. I wanted a response right away so I knew what he was thinking, but he truly did not know what to say.

I started to read his silence as being "disappointed in me" or "not wanting anything to do with me", so I also kept silent wallowing in my guilt.

He quietly said. "Angie, it doesn't matter to me what you've done in the past. I love you regardless." Tears flowed from my eyes. He forgave me.

There was still more to talk about though. He needed to know the importance of us waiting. I began to share with him about the book that my mom had given me, and how it had impacted my life. I told him that I thought it was important for us to stop being intimate, even kissing. He seemed a little confused at first but realized how important it was to me. He recognized what it was doing to our relationship, and how far we had gone. Even though we both enjoyed kissing, that night we made a pact that we would not continue to do it until we were married, if, of course, marriage was God's plan for us. I know, it sounds strange to think that we stopped kissing, but I knew what a simple kiss could lead to. I was not taking a risk with David. He was too special to me. This was the man that I wanted to be with the rest of my life.

Girl 2 girl chat

So many young women have come up to me since hearing my story asking me my opinion on the whole "kissing" thing. It is such a tough subject. I know that kissing can be innocent, but I also know that it can lead to destruction. I've seen it happen in my own life. A kiss can light you up inside. It literally gives you crazy tingling feelings that run straight through you. I believe that these feelings are a gift from God. They are not bad feelings. But I also believe that they can lead down a bad path if you are kissing when you really shouldn't be. I mean think about it. Why would you want to give away something so amazing as that electric kiss to just anyone? Can you imagine what it would feel like if you waited for your true love on your wedding day? Man, God would just floor you! He wants you to feel those rushes, but only at the right moment. And I believe the right moment is when you hear the words, "You may NOW kiss the bride".

Chapter Six

The Battle and the Proposal

Several months passed since David, and I had made the pact about "no kissing". Many times we wanted to go against our word, but we knew the importance of sticking with it. It was a constant battle. We tried to not be in situations where we would struggle. We spent a lot of time with other friends, and our time alone was always structured. No surprises. We knew that a night snuggling alone on the couch could lead to intimacy, so we avoided it, or we were with other couples snuggling in front of a movie.

We talked a lot about getting married, and we both knew that one day we would. God really had this relationship laid out for me. He knew what was best for me, and what I longed for.

When I think back, I wish that I would have realized it then. It would have saved me a lot of heartache, but once again, God knows the future and had a plan for all of this.

Girl 2 girl chat

In Ephesians 1:11 it says, "It's in Christ that we find out who we are, and what we are living for. Long before we first heard of Christ, he had his eye on us, had designs on us for glorious living, part of the overall purpose he is working out in everything and everyone."

Why do we fight God so much throughout our lives? He is the ultimate one in control.

We, as humans, are constantly trying to grab the steering wheel to control our destiny when it has already been decided for us. I would rather have someone higher and mightier than me directing my life. Why do I fight to control the outcome of things? I wanted popularity. He wanted me to be true to Him. I wanted to be pretty. He wanted me to see that I was beautiful and radiant. I wanted to be loved. He wanted me to feel how much He loved me, and that He gave His life for me. And yes, He wanted me to remain pure. To be patient for the godly man He had in store for me.

The letter

A year into our relationship David and I were having lunch at my house. We were watching a movie, sitting on the couch and eating a plate of my mom's delicious spaghetti once again. My parents came in and said that they were going for a drive. It's not unusual for my parents to go for a drive. They

Finding My Pure Heart Again

loved spontaneous trips to nowhere. The unusual part about it was they both came into the room smiling from ear to ear. Something was up. I brushed it off thinking that my parents were just slightly odd, and kept eating. After my mom and dad left, David got up and left the room. I love to eat so I just kept eating thinking he was going to use the restroom or something. He came back carrying a photo album that I had put together with pictures of us in it. He sat down next to me, and set aside my plate. "I guess I'm done with that." I joked.

He didn't laugh so I took a closer look at him, and he looked rather pale. I asked him if everything was okay. "Angie, I have loved every moment that we have had together. I made something for you." He nervously said. I opened the photo album feeling a little confused because I had actually made the album. What was he up to? He's re-gifting! I can't believe it! We sat and looked at the silly pictures that took us through our relationship together. I loved looking at them. When I reached the end of the book a letter was on the last few pages. I began to read. The words that followed were words that I wondered if I'd get a chance of ever hearing. He loved me more than his words could say. He wrote about some funny experiences that we've been through together over the last year, and I giggled with nervousness wondering where he was going with this. Then the ending of his letter said this…"the last year has brought us to where we are now…."

He got more and more pale. I looked more and more confused. Was he okay? Is this his way of

Finding My Pure Heart Again

breaking up with me? "Ang, will you marry me?" He asked as he pulled out a little grey box from his pocket.

What? He did not just ask me to marry him. Did he? I was still concerned about his appearance and really didn't notice the box or the question for that matter.

"Are you okay?" I asked as I noticed him shaking.

"Yes, yes, I'm better than okay...Ang, will you marry me?" he asked again.

I then grabbed him and held him tight. We both began to cry. We cried together for several minutes and David continued to shake. I truly was concerned about him. He asked me again, "Ang, I love you... will you marry me?"

Oh! He just proposed to me! Oh, he just proposed...was he kidding? He really wants to marry me? Me?

I yelled out," Yes, yes, of course I will!"

We sat together on my parent's couch. The very couch that we sat watching movies together, the couch where we shared our hearts, the couch where I shared with him my story of impurity, the couch where he offered his ever lasting love, the perfect place for a proposal.

I was shocked and overwhelmed. He loves me. This godly man that I desired for so long wants me to be his wife. He didn't care about the past. He loved me anyway, unconditionally.

Shortly after our tears dried, he handed me the small grey box again.

"You didn't even look at the ring that I gave you yet." He laughed.

I opened the box to reveal the most perfect ring, a ring that symbolizes everlasting love.

It was a moment that I will never forget.

My parents rushed in after an hour or so and began to share in our joy. They laughed at how long it took me to look at the ring. They shared with me a story of how David had met them several weeks prior to ask for my hand in marriage. I had no idea. We talked frequently about "when we get married" but never really said a date. Of course my mom stated several times how she was right, yes she was, and for once, I've never been more glad of that.

The Engagement

We set a date in October. We both loved the fall and thought that it would be a perfect time to visit the Smokey Mountains for a honeymoon.

Over the next months David and I struggled with wanting to get married sooner. We didn't really have a real reason why we wanted to move the date up, I think we were both just "ready". It seemed silly to wait. We'd known each other for years. We were friends. And it was difficult enough to wait on the kissing issue. Let's get this show on the road! Who planned this date any way, and why so far away?

After much prayer and guidance from friends, we decided to wait until the original date.

From that point on we counted the days.

Preparation for the Body, Mind & Soul

David and I spent the next few months in pre-marital counseling with a dear friend of ours. He was our worship pastor of our church for years and had known us both since we were very young. At first I didn't understand the importance of the counseling. I always thought people who needed help needed counseling. I'm glad that we took the time because I learned a lot about David. We enjoyed the time that we went to our sessions. It gave us a chance to open up and ask questions that we never thought about asking each other. It was a time of bonding. Plus, it helped remind us of the importance of waiting for intimacy. We were close to our wedding date, and it got more and more difficult to stay true to our commitment. We had to be careful. We were so close, only a couple more months.

Our counselor suggested that we meet with another married couple to interview them about their marriage. We selected a couple in our church whom we had known for years, and we planned a time to meet with them. They had been married for about 10 years, and they had two daughters. The couple invited us over for pizza one night. We didn't hold back. We needed to know the good and the bad. We wanted to know what to expect. What not to expect. We fired away the questions. They were honest and open and told us that marriage is not always easy. It takes two. Communication is the key.

David and I both learned a lot from that interview. We went home and decided to write up a marriage commitment. The commitment was actual things that we did and did not want to do in our marriage. After we had listed things that were important to us we both signed the bottom of the sheet and dated it. We placed it in a safe place until we could post it on our future refrigerator. It gave us a guide. It would help remind us in the upcoming years where we came from.

Girl 2 girl chat

Weddings and proms are so much alike. The dress, the flowers, the music, the dancing, and the food are all part of the special day. Yet, one huge difference is that prom lasts one evening. One moment and it is gone. A wedding also lasts only for one evening but the marriage should last a lifetime. I think many young girls spend so much time dreaming up their wedding day that they forget about what is really important. Yes, the wedding day is fun, and you'll never have a day quite like it again. It's exciting to pick out the dress, the flowers, the colors, the church, and the food. But what is truly important is preparing your mind for what you are about to do. Marriage is sacred. Marriage is forever. Marriage is a commitment between two people stating their love, and dedication to one another. Because today's world is so okay with divorce I think that marriage is looked at too lightly. It is so easy to just call it quits when things don't work out. But if you have your mind, and heart prepared that things are going to be hard, and you commit that divorce is NOT an option than you are truly ready for that big day.

It was the night of the rehearsal for our wedding. We had to "act" out walking down the aisle, saying the vows, and go over the flow of the wedding ceremony. I wasn't prepared for how I would feel looking into David's eyes as we stood at the altar. Here we were, standing face to face. I began to cry. Pure tears of joy. I felt pure happiness in the thought that it was David that I was marrying. And soon I could kiss him as my husband.

Chapter Seven

An October Wedding

My parents had just moved into this new home so my "temporary" room was nothing but a mattress on the floor. It was the night before my wedding day. I tossed and turned all night long. It was late, and I needed all the rest that I could get. The clock kept ticking, and I continued to lay awake. Moment by moment I pondered my life. Here I was, barely twenty, and I had experienced so much already. What more was there to come? Was I really getting married? The normal "plans" of the wedding day were not the topic of my thoughts. It was the struggles that I had faced. Will there ever be resolution there? Will I ever feel unashamed? No one but David knew about my past. I hid it from everyone.

Should I admit my sins to everyone so that I could feel totally forgiven? I knew that God had forgiven me, but will I really ever forgive myself? I'm about to venture into marriage. David and I will become one.

Finding My Pure Heart Again

The problem was that I had already been "one" with someone else. How do you fix that? Will there always be something between us that is unmentionable? All I knew was that I wanted David and I to come into this marriage pure. And we made it! We kept pure from one another, and we were finally going to have the freedom of intimacy within our marriage. What a beautiful and sacred concept. The way God intended. I went to the kitchen to grab a glass of milk when my mom walked in. She was concerned about me, and wondered why I was still up, and if everything was okay. We talked for awhile in the living room, and she stayed with me until we both eventually fell asleep. I woke only a couple hours later to a beautiful sunny October morning. I jumped in the shower to start my day. The hot water woke me up a bit, enough to allow me to function.

My wedding day, the most perfect day in my eyes. Margaret, my best friend, who I chose to be my maid of honor, picked me up as we headed to get our make-up done.

After arriving later to the church than we had planned, we quickly dressed, and did our hair. Everyone looked stunning. My mom and I began to get weepy as we looked at one another in the mirror. The photographer took every picture imaginable, and my mouth was already tired from smiling. I couldn't wait to see David. Was he nervous? Excited? Did he feel as much peace as I was feeling? This was what God had intended so there was never any feeling of doubt in my mind. All that I had to do was wait. Wait to see my groom.

Girl 2 girl chat

Isn't this what God does with us? He waits so patiently until we decide to meet him. He stands waiting as we awkwardly walk towards him. He lets us know that he is there but never steps on our toes, he just waits. He wanted me to finally, and completely come to Him, without any hesitation, without any doubt, without anything.

Desperate and lost I sought Him out again. And He was waiting for me with open arms.

Once again forgiving me, and welcoming me home.

When the time had finally come, I was ready to run down the aisle. But thankfully my

Dad kept a strong grip on my arm as we prepared to enter the sanctuary. He looked proud as he gazed at me. I wondered if he would be able to make it.

I asked him," Dad, are you okay?"

He smiled and replied, "Yes". That was all that I think he could say. We were both speechless. I didn't know who would be holding who up as we walked down the aisle.

The guests at our wedding stood as the wedding march sounded. This was our cue. I took a deep breath as my Dad and I took our first step, first step towards my prince, the one who I couldn't wait to spend the rest of my life with.

My Prince, Where is he?

Don't panic. He was there. But I could not see him. We had the little white church that I had wanted for our wedding day, but there was not a center aisle. I walked down the side aisle, and being that I was rather short, I could not see over all of my guests heads. So even though I wanted my gaze to be upon David, it was upon my family and friends. Then I finally came around the corner of the last pew, and there he stood. Pale as ever but he was standing upright. It was finally here. We were getting married. No more waiting. We could now begin our new lives together. No more struggles with not kissing. We could kiss as much as we wanted and then some. So, when was the pastor going to announce that we were husband and wife? It should be soon right?

My dad continued to hold unto my arm as the pastor prayed then he gave my hand to David. How symbolic. How beautiful of a sight. He gave permission, he handed me over to the man that I was to marry. I was no longer his little girl. I was a woman ready for the many years to come with my future husband. My dad kissed me, and headed to his seat beside my mom.

The pastor asked David and I to turn towards one another. I was finally going to get a good look at my groom. Wow. He looked perfect. His smile was soothing, and his heart leaped as he looked at me. It was almost as if we were the only two people in the room.

The pastor talked about how God had intended marriage, and how we are to approach it ourselves.

We exchanged rings, and began to light the unity candle. It was much like David to help me as I struggled to get the candle out of its holder. In fact, I almost had my dress and the entire sanctuary on fire if it wasn't for his help. He took it out for me, and helped me replace it again.

The service lasted for about a half hour until finally the pastor said these magical words...

You may NOW kiss your bride

It was a beautiful ceremony. There wasn't a dry eye in the church. Our guests were friends that we have both known for many years, We have been life long friends. I've known David since I was in 2nd grade, and he was in 5th grade. Who would have thought that we would be standing together at the altar preparing to venture into a life together hand in hand?

"You may NOW kiss your bride" the pastor happily said.

David looked at me like he never had before. I was his wife. He may kiss me now. He reached out, and put his hand on my cheek then he kissed me. It felt like it was the 1st kiss that I had ever received. Thank you Lord, we made it. The congregation cheered. We smiled at one another in disbelief.

"May I present to you, Mr. and Mrs. David Smith." the pastor announced.

David and I practically ran down the aisle. When we reached the end of the sanctuary we just embraced. David and Angie Smith. It was music to our ears. The photographer quickly caught us, and immediately started with the portfolio of pictures again. My mouth was hurting from all the pictures but I couldn't stop smiling.

After our guests had thrown all of the rice at us we headed to our horse drawn carriage that took us around the town square. It was intoxicating being in David's arms as his wife. We held each other the entire trip. People driving by honked, and waved wishing us luck. When we finally arrived at our reception hall all of our guests were already waiting for us. They announced us once again as we made our grand entrance. David and Angie Smith. We greeted everyone, and started the evening. We enjoyed a delicious meal that a friend of ours catered. We ate and ate and ate. I don't think any bride and groom ate as much as we did. We enjoyed our first meal together as husband and wife. We were interrupted several times by clanging of peoples spoons onto their glasses to imply us to kiss. Well, as you probably figured out, we didn't mind one bit. We just went right back to eating after giving them a good show.

The night continued with dancing. After the main festivities were over, we decided to sneak out of our own wedding for a walk around the hall. We had rented a lovely barn that was surrounded by a lake. It was the perfect location because the trees around the barn were starting to turn into their fall colors. We walked hand in hand just talking about the day, and how we both could not believe how we were now married.

Our photographer caught us as we were embraced admiring the sun setting from the day.

Finding My Pure Heart Again

It was the most perfect day in our eyes. A beautiful, October fall day. A wedding. A couple who had waited to get married, who had waited to kiss, who had waited for this moment. David and Angie Smith, husband and wife. The day had finally come.

Chapter Eight

Great Smoky Honeymoon and Ten Years After

After the guests had departed we said "goodnight" to our parents, and thanked them for all that they had done. We headed to the airport where we had to stay overnight at a hotel since our flight to Tennessee was early in the morning. We were both extremely tired but anticipated a romantic trip together, just the two of us as husband and wife. Our hotel room was a quaint suite with a fireplace. Because it was already late, we decided to get a small snack, and snuggle by the warm hearth.

After about an hour of reminiscing about the day we both agreed to continue the conversation in bed. The rest is history from there. I won't go into detail. But let me just say it was simply romantic and memorable. We both were glad that we had waited for this moment. Any thing short of that would not have been as special. This was the way God had intended.

When I was young my older brother and I used to "peek" at our Christmas presents. We knew just the right ways to gently unwrap them so that they would never suspect us as the culprits. It was exciting at the time, and it was a huge rush to "see" what was inside. But when Christmas morning came it just didn't seem as exciting. The thrill was gone. The moment has already taken place. It was already admired. The gift was already unveiled. The same is true for purity. If you've already experienced it, then the moment just isn't the same. Imagine if you've waited. The excitement, the thrill, the joy of unwrapping is so much greater.

Cabin on the Mountaintop

We arrived in Tennessee and drove our rental car through the mountains. It was an amazing site. We just kept driving further and further up. The winding roads made my stomach turn a bit, but the view kept getting more and more beautiful. When we finally reached the top there sat our cabin. Secluded and wooded at the top of what looked like the highest peak. It was breathtaking. The colors on the trees were just starting to turn, and the sun was on its way down. We ran into the cabin like two little kids. A kitchen, living room, fireplace, Jacuzzi for two and a very big bed was awaiting us to enjoy the entire week. Now, I say big bed because that is just what it was, big. It was slightly oversized, and droopy in the middle. I wonder if many other honeymooners have been here before us. We joked about that for awhile than decided to check out the view. We had a wrap around deck off of the back door that overlooked the mountain. There was nothing in site. I liked the thought of being in the middle of nowhere with my husband.

The rest of the week was magical. The time spent one on one was priceless. It's a shame honeymoons only last a week. I could have done this for an entire year. Getting to know

David this intimately was amazing. We enjoyed dinners by the fireplace, long talks on the deck, soaking in the Jacuzzi by candlelight, walks in the park, and many romantic nights and afternoons in the big droopy bed.

Chapter 8

My Guilty Conscience

The honeymoon came to an end, and David and I started our new life together. After a couple of years we decided it was time to purchase our 1st home. It was a fixer-upper but we loved it. When the weather got warmer we decided to landscape our yard. One Saturday we spent the entire day pulling weeds, planting, and digging holes.

We made several trips up to the local nursery to buy plants and equipment that we needed to finish the job. During one of our trips to the nursery; I was standing in line to check out, dirty clothes, dirty face, messy hair and all. Someone called my name. It was a familiar voice but I truly had no idea who it was.

"Angie?" the voice called again.

I turned and saw Gabe walking towards me.

I was surprised that I recognized him due to his shaved haircut. He had gone into the military over the last few years. He looked very clean cut and neat. Something at that moment I was not.

Now David was still shopping, so as you can imagine, I felt very awkward.

Gabe gave me a huge hug, and asked me how I was. I honesty don't even remember the conversation because I was shocked to see him. We chatted briefly until David stood by my side. They shook hands, and spoke kindly to one another. I felt relieved with David there, because I didn't know what stupid thing would come out of my mouth. Something like, "why don't you come over for dinner sometime". I've been known to say stupid things at the wrong time. Thankfully that comment never left my lips. After we said our goodbyes I felt a sense of guilt. I remember walking away to our car wondering what was he thinking about me. What was Gabe thinking, what was David thinking? Here was the guy that I had lost my virginity to. And there stood my husband. I almost wanted to apologize to David again, to once again ask him for forgiveness. On the other hand, I wanted to stop Gabe, and ask him for forgiveness for misleading him and not sharing my heart with him on how I felt about sex. I felt like I needed to apologize and tell him that I should never have had sex with him. That sex is for marriage. That night, unable to sleep, I tossed and turned wondering if I should do something about my feelings. David and I had several conversations over the whole "forgiveness" thing. He forgave me a long time ago, so that is not what was needed. So we decided that the best thing I could do was write to Gabe.

So that evening I spent writing a letter pouring out my heart about all that had happened to our relationship. Something I should have done after it happened. I shared with him some biblical truths about sex before marriage and how I wished that we hadn't done it. I shared with him that I felt like it had ruined our relationship and that it might ruin his relationship with his future wife. I basically told him that I was sorry for not being a better example. During our meeting he told me where his parents had moved to, which was close to our home. One day David and I drove past their home to get the address so that I could send the letter. As we drove past Gabe was walking the dog in their backyard.

David was sweet to suggest that I catch up with Gabe and hand it to him personally. I just didn't feel right about leaving my husband in the car so that I could talk to my ex-boyfriend. Instead of getting the address I just threw the letter in the mailbox. To this day, I don't know if Gabe read it, or what he thought of it, or if his parents read it. But that was my way of getting rid of my guilty conscience. Sad to say that it didn't work, I continued to feel guilt over my past and decided that it was just best to not talk about it or let anyone else know about it.

Intimacy

To be or not to be intimate…that is the question. I had always heard that when you have sex before marriage that you will forever be haunted of that past. I feared this with David.

I didn't want the thoughts of my past to hinder our sex life together. I wanted the story book romance, the hot sex I saw in movies, the sex that happened at any moment at any time. Wrong. It didn't happen this way. For reasons I did not understand I did not desire sex. Granted it was awesome. But I would never feel like initiating or go out of my way to even think about it. David is hot, don't get me wrong. He is everything I could ever dream of in a husband. I just wasn't feeling it. He would often wonder why I didn't initiate. He thought something was wrong with him. I never had a reason to why, in fact, I didn't even understand why. This is the man that God had brought to me, the man that I loved and treasured so much. What was wrong with me? Was my past hindering my sexual relationship with my husband now?

David and I both enjoyed the sex that we had but it seemed that it was always a "hot" topic that we both didn't really want to talk about. He would ask what was wrong and if I really wanted to "do it" and I would always say "of course" but again, I would never start the process. After almost six years of marriage, our first daughter, little Abigail came int the world. She was amazing and beautiful. Then two years following Abby came Isabelle.

Both girls added so much to our family, and we were thrilled to be parents. Unfortunately though our schedules became even more hectic, and our time together intimately became less and less. I didn't feel good in my new body (I called my once strong, firm stomach "my overstretched deflated tire belly"). I certainly did not think about sex after a long day of poopy diapers, bottles, and crying fits. And I did not understand why David would look at me the way that he did when my shirt came off.

Chapter Nine

The Topic of Sex

My friend Emily and I were talking one day when the subject came up about purity. She was involved in the teen ministry at our church, and they were planning an event for girls about self image, purpose and purity. I don't know why I but I began to share with her some of my experiences. She then asked me if I would be willing to speak to the teen girls about dating and boys. I am not a speaker. I get all mush mouthed, and nothing comes out right when I try. I took several public speaking courses but I could never get over the fear of being in front of people speaking from my heart. Strange thing about me is that I am an actress. I have always been the type that could get in front of a crowd, and act out just about anything. But speaking, having to be myself…not going to happen. So, this invitation was for me, out of the question. How could I get up in front of a bunch of girls, and share my story of dating? I had a bad experience, what would I say? "Well, I dated a lot of guys, and then I had sex" end of story. Oh, that's real encouraging! How could that help them? Then God talked to my heart. He wouldn't let this thing go. I had to speak to them. After several weeks of putting it off I sat down at my computer, and began to write. I needed this thing to be some what rehearsed. After the outline was done I read it to David who then said "you have to do this". That was that. I spoke in front of about 60 girls about boys, dating and purity. I shared my story, not in detail but I gave them the impression that I was not a virgin when I got married even though I never actually said it. I wasn't quite ready to do that. It was a stepping stone.

After I had finished speaking I challenged the girls to come, and talk with me. Several girls approached me, and said that my story really touched their hearts, and they wanted to remain pure until marriage. God had turned a bad experience in my life into something good. I could help other girls make better choices.

A small portion of my load was lifted. The next event would change my life forever…

Just a bunch of old women talking about sex
Well, my journey began, and before I knew it I was slowly becoming more and more willing to share my story. Emily who is founder and president of GodLight Ministries International had just started her ministry of reaching out to young women, and brought me along side of her to teach young girls about self-image, purpose and of course purity.

We traveled to different schools throughout Ohio teaching on these subjects. Another woman who joined our efforts in reaching young women was Joy. She had numerous experiences in speaking, and she added humor to her touching stories on purity. I stuck to writing, directing and occasionally acting in the dramas that we would perform. I wasn't ready to speak. One day Joy approached Emily and I with the thought of going to a seminar for women. She convinced us that the seminar would help us polish off our speaking skills, and would allow us to see how other women speak at these types of events. The speakers were two women who had written a book on none other than…sex.

"Are you kidding," I said to Emily one day, "I am not going to a seminar with a bunch of old women talking about sex!"

She agreed, and we went on our way.

Joy brought it up again.

"Come on guys, the seminar is this weekend, and there are some tickets left. It will give us some great ideas on how we should do things." Joy continued to encourage.

"Alright, I'll go, but I will not enjoy it!" I jokingly said.

All week long I dreaded going to the seminar. I was going for "research" purposes only.

I certainly was not going to actually learn anything from this. I knew sex. I didn't need to know any thing more about it. And I didn't need two old women telling me about it.

The weekend came. I picked up Emily and we headed to the seminar. We both joked about how we were "persuaded" to go by Joy, and we would let her know how unhappy we were going to be the entire day.

When we arrived Joy had saved us seats next to several other women that we knew from our church. I was so embarrassed. I was hoping that no one would see me. Let alone two rows of women from our church. Ughhhhh.

The day started out with singing, and then a girl performed a drama on sex. I have to admit it was a clever skit on how sex is perceived. Then the speakers took their places.

What in the world did these women have to say about sex that would last an entire seminar? I sighed thinking it was going to be a very long two days. The speakers opened up with prayer, and encouraged us to say a short prayer that went like this," Lord, I am here for a reason, open up my heart to your words."

I hesitated. Yes, in fact I was here for a reason. Joy made me come. But I prayed the Prayer, and the day began.

As the speakers started, right away I liked their style of speaking. I quickly got out my Notepad, and began to jot down ideas to how we can run our future speaking conferences.

They used humor, and they tag teamed the topics. They also used images, cartoon clippings, music, video…any media you can think of, they used it. It kept the sessions interesting. It interested me more than I would have thought it ever could, so I listened, and took less notes.

First they spoke about how image is portrayed in today's media, then how sex is portrayed. That movies and television shows make sex out to be this awesome, romantic, natural, non-stop event that two people experience at the drop of a hat! What? Come on!

When has this truly ever happened?

"Hi honey, how was your day at work?" he says as his wife walks in from a hard day.

"Not as good as this is going to be!" She replies ripping the buttons off of his shirt.

This type of crazy sex usually does not occur everyday in marriage. Only in the movies.

I was listening now. This is how I felt. I certainly did not look or feel as sexy as those women on television and the movies. I never felt the desire to rip off my husbands shirt as I walked in the house from work. But this is how the world made it appear. The world made sex out to be a free for all, at all times, at any moment experience that if you didn't do this at home, there must be something wrong with you. Then most couples separate thinking it will be better with someone else.

Thankfully, I never got into soap operas. I always felt that they were fake, first of all, who looks that good just getting out of bed, and secondly everyone slept with everyone, and they all lived in the same town. Most importantly though, sex is portrayed so falsely, it doesn't just come at the chime of a bell or when a single candle is lit.

Making sense of it all

I agreed with these ladies. I knew what they were saying. This is how the world sees sex.

Then how is it supposed to really be? How does God see sex?

Then they began to tell me. Not only is an entire book of the Bible dedicated to the subject but God wants us to do it. He created us to do it. It says in his word that," the two shall become one". In the book of Song of Songs it says that we are to fully enjoy it. The speakers explained that God intended sex to be for marriage only, and that those who were doing it outside of that were sinning. Again, I knew this. But how do you break free from something that happened in the past?

Then they began to tell me.

At this point, I swore that this seminar was just for me.

The speaker asked each of us to close our eyes. She told us to imagine a garden, a beautiful, colorful garden with many flowers and lush plants. She then had us go back to our childhood, as young as we can remember. Then she asked when we first discovered the word sex. Was it on a playground? Was it from a kid in your neighborhood? She told us to replace one of those plants with a weed. Then she asked us when we first talked about sex. Was it with a friend? Replace another plant with a weed. Then she asked us if we remembered our first kiss. Was it a good experience? Did you do it on a dare? Were you pressured to do it? Replace another plant with a weed. Then she asked if we remember ever being violated sexually. Was it with a kid on the bus, or an uncle, or a close family friend? Replace another. Then she told us to think over our teenage years.

What are some of the events that we remember? Did we get intimate with our first serious boyfriend? Another weed. Did you let your boyfriend touch you? Weed. Did you come close to sex? Weed. Did you have sex? Weed.

Weed, after weed, after weed. My mind began to spin. I literally saw my life flash before me as she spoke.

The kids at school talking about sex, the images on television, the magazines, the dare on the back of a bus that pressured me into French kissing a boy, the serious boyfriend at age 14, the make-out session with the boy that I didn't even like, the overnight with my boyfriend. Then the final image that I saw was my last night of purity. I became disgusted. Tears were flowing from my eyes.

The huge, ugly weed

The speaker continued, and told us to look over our garden. My beautiful garden was now a pile of weeds, dirt everywhere, no sign of life in it at all. She then had us imagine one huge weed in the middle of our garden that reached up to the sky. She told us to grab it, to try to take hold of it. In my mind I grabbed at that thing with all of my might. But then she said that the weed will not move. I imagined myself pulling and pulling at that huge ugly weed, but she was right, it didn't budge. Then she said that

Finding My Pure Heart Again

there was a way to get it out. What, a way to remove this shameful disgusting weed, how?

Ask God to remove it. Take it before Him, and let Him yank it out. There is nothing else to do but surrender it to Him.

The tears continued to flow. I knew what she meant. All of these years I have been disobeying God, and his plan for purity for me. I asked for forgiveness years ago, but had never forgiven myself. This was the time.

The speaker asked us to come forward if we needed to remove this sin in our lives. I have never been so quick on my feet. I opened my eyes, and headed to the front stage. I didn't care who was sitting next to me or who saw me admit my failures. It was between me and God. I fell to my knees and sobbed. The speaker continued talking. She asked the rest of the people sitting in their seats to pray for those of us who had come forward.

We sat and prayed which seemed like just moments. That is when I realized how many women I was surrounded by. Many others just like me had come forward bowing at the feet of Christ, asking him to remove the weeds in their lives. I have never heard such a sound of women sobbing. In unison, we cried and prayed. God must have leaped knowing that each of us had finally surrendered to Him. As tissue was being passed, the speaker once again began to speak. She prayed that God would remove that huge, ugly weed in our garden, and replace it with the beautiful flowers again. That he would make us pure again.

Then when her prayer had finished, the wildest thing happened. The sobs stopped. My tears stopped flowing. The women next to me stopped crying. It was like God calmed our sorrows, and wiped the slate clean again.

With my head bowed I began to smile. I found peace. Peace that I hadn't felt in a long time.

The speaker asked us to go back to our seats. As I rose up from the ground, I noticed the burden lifted. My weed was removed.

Girl 2 girl chat

Forgiveness, that is what God has given. He wanted me to forgive myself, to fully give the sin to Him. To surrender my life completely I had to let Him take that huge, ugly weed from me. I didn't realize that He had already taken it, but I continued to see it because I never forgave myself. He forgave me years ago. I just needed to open my eyes to the gift of forgiveness that He so freely gave.

Chapter Ten

The Joy of Sex finally revealed

The day had ended and the seminar came to a close. I thanked Joy for persuading me to attend. She had listened to God pushing her to push me to hear these women speak. Boy, am I glad that she did. I felt like a new women. The seminar involved many other points that touched and educated me but most of all it gave me the opportunity to see what my problem was.

I never truly forgave myself so I never felt completely cleansed of my sin.

This way of thinking trickled down into my love life with my husband, and caused me to not enjoy sex the way that God had intended. He intended it for good. He wants and desires me to have a wonderful, adventurous sex life with my husband. Now that I have seen this and what it has done to me I was ready to make things different.

Wrapped with a red ribbon

When I had arrived home that evening I knew that David and I would have to talk. I didn't want to wait. If he knew what he was in for he wouldn't want to wait! After putting the kids to bed I quickly ran around the house in search of some red ribbon. The speakers came up with this idea, and encouraged us to mimic what they had done for their spouses.

At first I thought it was a crazy but I also felt like it was a new beginning so I did it anyway. After locating the ribbon I undressed, and wrapped myself up in it. Yep, that's right, I wrapped myself up in red ribbon and nothing else. Sounds silly? It was. I felt silly.

But I wanted him to know how I felt, and what it meant. When David was finished with his shower he was pleasantly surprised to see me. He looked a little confused but intrigued. I then began to tell him about the seminar and explained to him why I was dressed in this manner, or lack there of. I told him that I finally felt free of my past and was ready to start over with him. I admitted that our sex life wasn't what it should be, and that I desired it to be. I told him that I had worn the red ribbon to simplify that I was a gift wrapped especially for him and him only. I was giving myself to him. My new found purity made me desire intimacy more, and I told him that from now on it would be different.

His eyes welled up. He was speechless. He, like myself had no idea how the seminar would have impacted me. We embraced and continued to talk. I told him about my huge, ugly weed and how God had removed it, and how the burden of my past was erased for good.

He could not have been anymore happy for me. He knew it had affected our relationship.

We both had, but never wanted to admit it or bring up the subject.

After we shed several tears I reminded him of the fact that I was still only dressed in red ribbon. He smiled at the thought, and gladly removed it. We then shared in what felt like our first night together as husband and wife. In fact, it was like I had never experienced it before.

Our New Life
Over the next several months our marriage began to change. We became closer than we had ever experienced before. It took us ten years of marriage to get to this point, but that seminar had changed it for good. We were not going back to the old way. Our marriage was always good, and we had many good times together, but it was now at a stage that it had never been. I praise God for taking me into the place where I did not really want to venture into. Had He not taken me there my marriage may have slowly gone down the tubes.

I know that God has given me a new found love for David. A sexual love for him that I didn't know existed. I learned at the seminar that yes men and women are made differently, and we just aren't wired to think about sex as much as men. But God can clear your mind and give you those exciting feelings for a beautiful sex life if you simply ask. My mind was not clear, it had junk and dirt covering the beauty of sex that God had intended for me.

Let me explain something before this book ends. I don't want anyone to think that everything was peachy and perfect from that moment on. It wasn't. David and I still have to make time for one another physically. I don't rip his clothes off when he enters the house after work, even though it would be fun to see his face if I would do that. Sex is sometimes spontaneous but most of the time it is planned. We have kids. We can't just run around the house naked! We set aside special time, and plan our intimacy. It gives the experience a little bit of wonder and anticipation.

If you are married: don't let the world of movies and soap operas deceive you into believing that sex is always perfect and passionate. It takes two to tango and most of the time you don't know the steps.

There is not a director telling you what to do next. You and your spouse will probably fumble through sex until you figure each other out. Now, don't be discouraged either. Sex is wonderful. It just takes time to know how each other ticks, and what is best for you and your marriage partner. Enjoy your intimacy. Read Song of Solomon before entering into intimacy, it gives you many ideas of how to love and romance your spouse.

Another good idea for married couples it to get <u>Simply Romantic Nights</u> by Linda Dillow and Lorraine Pintus. It will ignite your marriage!

If you are NOT married: I challenge you, if you are currently in a relationship that is sexual, please stop the intimacy immediately. Your partner will understand if they truly love you. Like David, they will wait for you. They will be willing to wait until you are both married if they are seriously into you as a person. If they refuse and don't want to wait then I question their dedication and love. You then should question it too. You should also question why you are IN the relationship. If you are filling a void in your life to make you feel loved then try seeking out your Creator first. He is the true lover of your soul. He may not be here physically, but He can capture your heart strings like no other, filling that void. He says that He will never leave us or forsake us. Now you tell me, what earthly relationship can do that?

My Pure Heart

God showed me that I could still become pure even though I had lost my purity. All of those years that I had held onto my sin, caused my heart to be far from God. I didn't know it at the time, but Satan was slowly pushing me away. Satan wanted me to hide my past, to bury it, and not let anyone know about it. So I continued to carry the burden until God broke through, and revealed to me what I was carrying on my back. When the sin was finally admitted and completely given to God I could be set free of the burden. Free of the weeds! Free of the shame! Revealing a lovely, beautiful, clean garden where God was going to do a mighty work in. Now I can walk through my garden and no longer feel the shame and disgust of seeing my past and despising the weeds that overtook it. I can gaze upon the beauty that God has restored. I have found my pure heart again.

> *When I kept silent, my bones wasted away through my groaning all day long. For day and night your hand was heavy on me; my strength was sapped as in the heat of summer.*
> ***Then I acknowledged my sin to you*** *and did not cover up my iniquity. I said, "I will confess my transgressions to the Lord"* — ***and you forgave the guilt of my sin****.*
> *- Psalm 32: 3-5*

For more information on Angie's ministry *PurityTalks*, or to have her visit your youth group or retreat to chat on self image, dating and purity, check out her blog at www.puritytalks.blogspot.com

LaVergne, TN USA
30 September 2010

199080LV00001B/2/P